peter popple's

popcorn
cookbook

Published in 2012 by Short Books
3a Exmouth House
Pine Street
EC1R 0JH
1 2 3 4 5 6 7 8 9 10

Copyright © Louise George 2012

A CIP catalogue record for this book is available from the British Library.

Picture Credits:
Peter Popple's branding © Family (and friends)
Photography © Romas Foord
Images on p 36, 43, 46, 52,59 & 89 © Shutterstock ltd

ISBN 978-1-78072-030-2

Printed by Hung Hing, China

peter popple's
popcorn
cookbook

Come on in to find delicious popcorn recipes, facts and more!

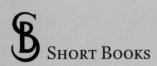
SHORT BOOKS

contents

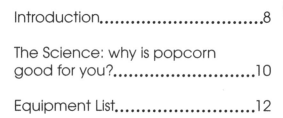

sweet popcorn

savoury popcorn

Introduction

Welcome to the Peter Popple's Popcorn Cookbook! My name is Peter Popple, and I'm a young scientist who loves everything that goes **pop!** and the science behind it. Of all of my experiments, my favourite is making the perfect popcorn.

I live in a barn with a special 'popping' kitchen where I make all my popcorn. In this cookbook, I have written down all of my favourite recipes so that you can have fun making popcorn of your own, with friends and family.

Popcorn is a versatile and creative food, whether you are looking for party food or a snack for your lunchbox. And adults like it too!

So how does popcorn work? Well, each kernel (grain) of popcorn contains a certain amount of moisture, oil and starch. Unlike most other grains, the outside of the popcorn kernel is very strong. When the kernel is heated to a high temperature (more than 180°C), the water inside the kernel expands, makes a popping sound and the starch inside is turned into the popcorn puff as it breaks through the wall of the kernel.

This 'popping' can be done in an 'air popper' machine in which the heated air is circulated to keep the un-popped kernels in motion and stop them burning. This is a healthy way of cooking popcorn as it uses no oil.

You can also cook popcorn by putting your kernels, together with a small amount of oil or butter, in a saucepan with the lid on (to stop your popcorn escaping!). You then put this over a medium heat. The oil/butter helps transfer the heat to make the popcorn go 'pop'. You can also buy microwaveable popcorn – simply follow the instructions on the packet.

Once you have popped your popcorn, you can have fun adding all the different ingredients I have suggested to create **popalicious popcorn!**

THE SCIENCE:

Why is popcorn good for you?

Popcorn is a wholegrain and has a low GI number, keeping you fuller for longer. It is also full of antioxidants and B vitamins to boost your energy levels.

How healthy the popcorn is depends on how much butter/oil and flavourings you use – some of our recipes are better for you than others, so some should be eaten in moderation (a grown up's way of saying don't eat it all day every day!) while others you can have more often – but they all taste delicious!

EQUIPMENT LIST

Air popper (you can use a saucepan if you don't have an air popper. See instructions on how to do this on page 16)

(See instructions on how to do this on page 16)

Bowl for popped popcorn

Saucepan (medium size)

Wooden spoon for mixing

Tablespoon and teaspoon for measuring ingredients

Cheese grater

Mixing bowl

Knife – Remember! You should always be supervised by an adult when using a knife

---

Ovenproof tin (8–10 inch)

Food processor/blender (for some recipes)

Rolling pin (for some recipes)

Paper cake cases (for some recipes)

Ice cream maker (for one recipe)

Instructions for using an air popcorn popper machine

1 Plug in air popcorn popper machine.

2 Place large bowl under spout

3 Measure out popcorn kernels and place in popper

4 Turn on machine, wait (the machine may take a short while to warm up) and watch popcorn pop into bowl

5 When all kernels have popped, turn off machine

6 Remove any un-popped kernels from the bowl

Instructions for making popcorn on the stove

1. Pour in enough oil to coat the bottom of the pan.

2. Place a couple of kernels in the oil, and put the pan over a medium heat.

3. When the kernels begin to pop, add the rest of your kernels (enough to cover the bottom of the pan, no more than one kernel deep is best), replace the lid of the pan, and let the popcorn pop!

4. When the sound of the popcorn popping starts to slow down, remove your pan from the heat, and you should have a pan of deliciously popped popcorn, ready to use in the recipes that follow.

Important! You <u>must</u> have an adult with you when making popcorn in a pan.

NOTE: All recipes use 50g of popcorn kernels which makes enough popcorn for 3-4 children/adults.

sweet
popcorn

Nutty 'n' Natural Popcorn

50g of popcorn kernels
1 tablespoon of sunflower seeds
1 tablespoon of almonds, finely ground
1 tablespoon of walnuts or hazelnuts, finely ground
1 tablespoon of butter
A pinch of salt

Air pop popcorn using an air popper machine (see pages 15-18 for instructions), put in large bowl and set aside.

Finely grind sunflower seeds and nuts in a food processor or blender.

Melt butter over a low heat on a stove, pour melted butter over popcorn and add salt.

Sprinkle ground nuts over popcorn, toss to mix and coat evenly.

Great for serving at children's parties!

POP FACT:
When they are popping, popcorn kernels can reach a height of three feet!

Peanut Butter Popcorn

50g of popcorn kernels
1 tablespoon of butter
1 tablespoon of smooth peanut butter

Air pop popcorn using an air popper machine (see pages 15-18 for instructions), put in large bowl and set aside.

In a medium-sized pan, melt the butter and the peanut butter over a low heat, stiring continuously.

Pour this mixture over the popcorn, stir well and serve immediately.

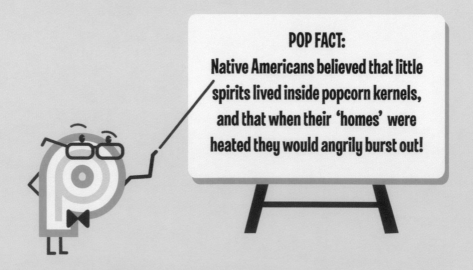

POP FACT:
Native Americans believed that little spirits lived inside popcorn kernels, and that when their 'homes' were heated they would angrily burst out!

Cinnamon (Apple) Popcorn

50g of popcorn kernels
2 tablespoons of chopped dried
   apples – optional
2 tablespoons of pecan halves
   (roughly chopped) – optional

2 tablespoons of butter
1 teaspoon of cinnamon powder
¼ teaspoon of nutmeg
2 teaspoons of brown sugar
¼ teaspoon of vanilla extract

Air pop popcorn using an air popper machine (see pages 15-18 for instructions), put in large bowl and set aside.

In a medium-sized saucepan, melt the butter on a low heat.

Add cinnamon, brown sugar, nutmeg and vanilla to melted butter and stir for one minute until well blended. (Add chopped dried apples and chopped pecan halves now if using.)

Add popcorn to the pan, stir well and serve immediately.

Great for serving at children's parties!

POP FACT:
Corn is a member of the grass family of plants, but more tasty (unless you are a cow, of course).

Marmalade Popcorn Balls

(Makes 10-12 balls)

50g of popcorn kernels
1 tablespoon of sugar
2 tablespoons of water
2 tablespoons of orange marmalade

A pinch of salt
1 tablespoon of golden syrup
1 teaspoon of vinegar
25g of butter

Air pop popcorn using an air popper machine (see pages 15-18 for instructions), put in large bowl and set aside.

Combine sugar, water, marmalade, salt, golden syrup and vinegar in a medium-sized saucepan; bring to the boil, and stir until the sugar dissolves.

Continue to heat until the mixture is of a thick consistency.

Pour mixture over the popcorn slowly, then mix thoroughly.

Leave to cool for a few minutes.

Spoon mixture into cake cases, shaping mixture into balls as you do so.

Allow to cool for a further half an hour before serving.

CORNY JOKE:
What did the
Baby Corn say to the
Mummy Corn?
"Where's Pop Corn?"

Choc-toffee Drizzle Popcorn Bars

Makes 6 large toffee popcorn bars

50g of popcorn kernels
2 tablespoons of chopped, roasted and salted peanuts
2 tablespoons of desiccated coconut (to be toasted)

For the toffee:
2 tablespoons of butter
2 tablespoons of brown sugar
3 tablespoons water
2 tablespoons of golden syrup

For the chocolate topping:
50g of chocolate (milk or dark depending on preference) or chocolate buttons

Preheat the oven to 130°C.

Air pop popcorn using an air popper machine (see pages 15-18 for instructions), put in large bowl and set aside.

Lay coconut on baking tray and bake for 10 minutes or until golden.

Combine popcorn, peanuts and toasted coconut in a large bowl.

Cover the bottom of a buttered 8-10 inch tin with half of the popcorn mixture.

Set aside the remaining popcorn mixture – to be added later.

For the toffee sauce: Important! Please ensure that you have an adult with you when making toffee as the mixture can get very hot and be extremely dangerous.

Melt butter over a low heat in a large saucepan.

Add sugar and blend well. Continue to cook over low heat, stirring constantly, until mixture reaches boiling point.

Add water and golden syrup to the butter/sugar and mix well to make toffee.

Immediately pour the toffee over the popcorn in the tin, making certain it is well covered.

Quickly spread the remaining popcorn mixture on top of this and press it into the hot toffee. Set aside to cool.

For the chocolate topping:

Melt the chocolate in a bowl over a saucepan of boiling water.

Drizzle melted chocolate over the toffee-popcorn mixture in tin.

Allow to cool. Cut into bars.

POP FACT:
Popcorn is a Snack
of All Trades!
Popcorn has more
phosphorus,
protein and iron
than an ice cream
cone, pretzels
or crisps!

Baked Caramel Popcorn

50g of popcorn kernels
2 tablespoons of butter
2 tablespoons of brown sugar
1 tablespoon of golden syrup

A pinch of salt
$\frac{1}{2}$ teaspoon of baking soda
1 teaspoon of vanilla extract

Air pop popcorn using an air popper machine (see pages 15-18 for instructions), put in large bowl and set aside.

Melt butter over low heat and then stir in brown sugar, golden syrup and salt.

Bring to the boil, stirring constantly. Continue to boil without stirring for 5 minutes. (Again, you <u>must</u> have an adult with you when making this one).

Remove from heat and stir in baking soda and vanilla extract.

Gradually pour over popcorn, mixing well.

Turn into an 8-10 inch buttered tin.

Bake at 130°C for one hour, stirring every 15 minutes.

Remove from oven.

Cool completely. Break apart and enjoy!

It's chewy!

Fruity Baked Popcorn

50g of popcorn kernels
1 tablespoon of glazed red
   cherries or other dried fruit,
   chopped
1 tablespoon of chopped pecans

1 tablespoon of brown sugar
2 tablespoons of butter
3 tablespoons of golden syrup
$1/4$ teaspoon of baking soda
$1/4$ teaspoon of vanilla extract

Air pop popcorn using an air popper machine (see pages 15-18 for instructions), put in large bowl and set aside.

Combine popcorn with cherries/dried fruit and pecans, and place in an 8-10 inch baking tray.

In a medium-sized saucepan, combine sugar, butter and golden syrup and stir over low heat until butter melts and mixture begins to bubble.

Continue to stir over low heat for a further five minutes. Remove from heat. Stir in baking soda and vanilla extract.

Pour mixture over popcorn in baking tray and gently stir to coat.

Bake at 130°C for 15 minutes, then remove from oven, and stir popcorn mixture again. Bake for a further 5 to 10 minutes. Cool, then cut into squares.

Toffee Apple Popcorn

50g of popcorn kernels
2 tablespoons of chopped apple rings
Toffee sauce (see directions
   for making toffee in Choc-toffee
   Drizzle Popcorn Bars on pages 28-29)

Air pop popcorn using an air popper machine (see pages 15-18
for instructions), put in large bowl and set aside.

Make toffee sauce (as before).

Add chopped apples to toffee sauce and stir.

Finally stir in popcorn, mix well and serve.

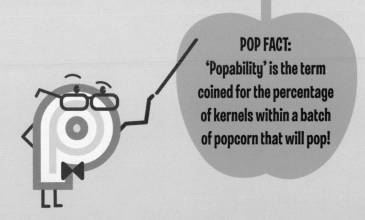

POP FACT:
'Popability' is the term
coined for the percentage
of kernels within a batch
of popcorn that will pop!

Pop-a-rific Popcorn Balls

50g of popcorn kernels
50g of marshmallows
2 tablespoons of butter

Air pop popcorn using an air popper machine (see pages 15-18 for instructions), put in large bowl and set aside.

In a medium-sized saucepan, melt marshmallows and butter over a low heat until smooth.*

Pour marshmallow mixture over the popcorn, tossing gently to mix well.

Allow to cool for 10 minutes.

Butter hands well and form 2 $1/2$ inch balls (about the size of golf balls).

*To colour the popcorn balls, add a few drops of food colouring to the smooth marshmallow mixture. You can always divide the mixture into 2 or 3 bowls and use 2 or 3 different food colours to make your popcorn balls more exciting!

White Chocolate Popcorn

50g of popcorn kernels
50g of white chocolate or white chocolate buttons

Air pop popcorn using an air popper machine (see pages 15-18 for instructions), put in large bowl and set aside.

Break white chocolate into pieces if using bars and put in bowl. Melt on low heat over pan of boiling water.

Drizzle white chocolate over popcorn.

Leave for 15 minutes to harden before serving.

POP FACT:
In popcorn jargon, a popped kernel of corn is known as a 'flake' and an irregular flake is called a 'butterfly'.

Popcorn Jelly Cakes

(Makes 10-12 servings)

50g of popcorn kernels
50g of marshmallows
2 tablespoons of butter
1 packet of mini jelly babies (or large jelly babies, chopped small)
1 tablespoon of chopped peanuts

Air pop popcorn using an air popper machine (see pages 15-18 for instructions), put in large bowl and set aside.

In a medium-sized saucepan, melt marshmallows and butter over a low heat until smooth.

Add jelly babies and peanuts to bowl of popcorn and mix.

Add marshmallow mixture to popcorn and mix well.

Press into a greased 8-10 inch cake tin or into cake cases. Cover and refrigerate for five hours or overnight.

If using cake tin, place pan in shallow bowl of hot water (without allowing water to enter tin!) for five to ten seconds to loosen cake from mold. Slice cake with a serrated knife, and serve.

Popcorn Ice Cream (with Hot Chocolate Sauce)

NOTE: You will need an ice cream maker for this recipe.

50g of popcorn kernels
300ml of full-fat milk
300ml of double cream
150g of caster sugar
1/2 tsp of pure vanilla extract
1 egg

For the Chocolate Sauce (optional):
75g of dark or milk chocolate
125ml of double cream
1 tablespoon of Golden Syrup

Air pop popcorn using an air popper machine (see pages 15-18 for instructions), put in large bowl and set aside.

Heat the milk, cream, popcorn and half of the sugar in a saucepan until it's just below boiling point and starts to bubble.

Remove and then allow to sit for 30 minutes so that the popcorn has thoroughly infused its flavour into the cream mixture.

Strain the mixture through a fine sieve.

Whisk together the other half of the sugar, vanilla and egg in a bowl until the mixture is pale and thick.

Still whisking, pour the cream mixture into the egg mixture. Pour this back into a pan and stir over a low heat until it thickens to a velvety, custard consistency.

Remove from the heat. Pour into a bowl and allow to cool.

Churn in an ice cream maker, according to manufacturer's instructions.

To make the chocolate sauce:

Break up the chocolate, put into a medium-sized saucepan and melt over a low heat.

Add the cream and Golden Syrup, and continue to stir.

Once everything has melted together, remove pan from the heat and pour the chocolate sauce into a jug, to serve with the ice cream.

These popcorn bars are great as an afternoon treat or to be served at parties!

Blueberry Oat Popcorn Bars

50g of popcorn kernels
50g of coarsely chopped dry-
  roasted peanuts
50g of dried blueberries
  (cranberries will work too)

50g of uncooked oats
50g of marshmallows
2 tablespoons of butter
1 tablespoon of honey

Air pop popcorn using an air popper machine (see pages 15-18 for instructions), put in large bowl and set aside.

Add peanuts, berries and oats to popcorn and mix together.

In a medium-sized saucepan, melt marshmallows, butter and honey over a low heat.

Pour marshmallow mixture over popcorn mixture and stir until completely coated.

Grease an 8-10 inch pan with butter and press popcorn mixture into pan.

Refrigerate until set, about one hour should do. Cut into bars. Store in an airtight container if not being eaten immediately.

Chocolate Chilli Popcorn

50g of popcorn kernels
1 tablespoon of icing sugar
$^1/_2$ tablespoon of milk powder
1 tablespoon of cocoa powder
A pinch of chilli powder (mild)
Cooking oil spray

Air pop popcorn using an air popper machine (see pages 15-18 for instructions), put in large bowl and set aside.

In a bowl, combine icing sugar, milk powder, cocoa powder and chilli powder.

Lightly mist popcorn with the cooking oil spray. This is to help the mixture hold together.

Sprinkle on the chocolate/chilli mix and stir well before serving.

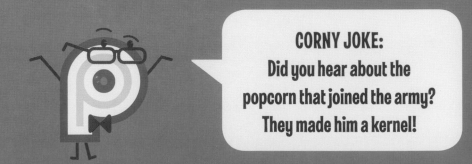

CORNY JOKE:
Did you hear about the
popcorn that joined the army?
They made him a kernel!

Yummy Yoghurt Popcorn

50g of popcorn kernels
500g of plain (preferably Greek-style)
   yoghurt
2 tablespoons of runny honey
A handful of dried fruit (seeds and
   nuts optional)

Air pop popcorn using an air popper machine (see pages 15-18 for instructions),
put in large bowl and set aside.

In a medium-sized mixing bowl, combine yogurt, honey, dried fruit and popcorn.

Serve in individual bowls – ideal for breakfast.

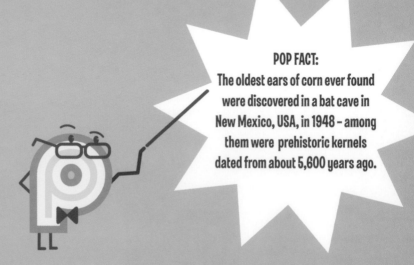

POP FACT:
The oldest ears of corn ever found
were discovered in a bat cave in
New Mexico, USA, in 1948 – among
them were prehistoric kernels
dated from about 5,600 years ago.

Popcorn Crispy Cakes

50g of popcorn kernels
50g of marshmallows
2 tablespoons of Golden Syrup
50g of milk chocolate

Air pop popcorn using an air popper machine (see pages 15-18 for instructions), put in large bowl and set aside.

Gently heat the marshmallows, milk chocolate and golden syrup in a bowl over a pan of water until softened, stirring continuously.

Spoon the mixture over the popcorn and mix well.

Spoon into cake cases and refrigerate.

TIP: Wash your pan and mixing bowl with hot water immediately after use – this will make cleaning them much easier than if you allow the marshmallow and syrup to harden!

Great for serving at children's parties!

Bounty Popcorn

50g of popcorn kernels
1 large bag/3 small bags of chocolate buttons
2 tablespoons of desiccated coconut

Air pop popcorn using an air popper machine (see pages 15-18 for instructions), put in large bowl and set aside.

Warm chocolate buttons in a bowl over a pan of water on a low heat.

Once chocolate is melted, stir in coconut and remove from heat.

Pour chocolate/coconut mixture over popcorn and mix well.

Serve immediately.

Sticky Strawberry Popcorn

50g of popcorn kernels
2 tablespoons of strawberry jam
2 tablespoons of water
1 tablespoon of Golden Syrup

Air pop popcorn using an air popper machine (see pages 15-18 for instructions), put in large bowl and set aside.

Combine strawberry jam, water and Golden Syrup in a saucepan over a low heat.

Remove from heat, add mixture to popcorn and stir well.

Leave to cool, then serve.

POP FACT:
Corn is produced on every continent of the world except Antarctica (a shame for all you popcorn-loving penguins!)

Banoffee Toffee Popcorn

50g of popcorn kernels
2 tablespoons of dried banana chips
Toffee sauce (see directions for making toffee in
   Choc-toffee Drizzle Popcorn Bars on pages 28-29)

Air pop popcorn using an air popper machine (see pages 15-18 for instructions), put in large bowl and set aside.

Make toffee sauce (as before).

Put banana chips in food/freezer bag, seal and use rolling pin to crush.

Stir toffee sauce into popcorn, then add the crushed banana chips and stir again well.

Spoon the mixture into paper cup cases. These can be eaten warm or allowed to cool in the fridge.

Great for serving at children's parties!

POP FACT:
Corn plants range in height from five to seven feet, roughly the same height as most grown-ups.

savoury popcorn

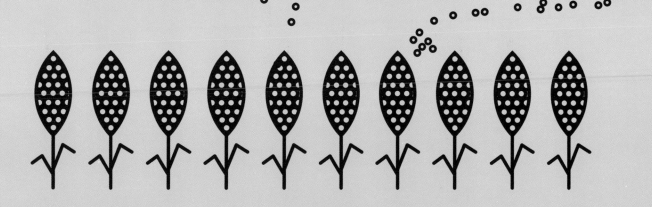

Marmite popcorn

50g of popcorn kernels
1 tablespoon of butter
1 teaspoon of Marmite

Air pop popcorn using an air popper machine (see pages 15-18 for instructions), put in large bowl and set aside.

Melt tablespoon of butter in a medium-sized saucepan over a stove on a low heat.

When butter is almost melted, add teaspoon of Marmite. Mix well with wooden spoon.

Add mixture to air popped popcorn, stir well and serve immediately.

POP FACT:
Researchers believe that 5,000 years ago, cave people most likely used to eat popcorn as a snack!

Italian Popcorn

50g of popcorn kernels
2 tablespoons of grated Parmesan cheese
1 teaspoon of Italian herb seasoning
Cooking oil spray

Air pop popcorn using an air popper machine (see pages 15-18 for instructions), put in large bowl and set aside.

Place grated Parmesan cheese in a bowl and mix in Italian herb seasoning.

Spray popcorn lightly with cooking oil spray, toss with the mixture of Parmesan and seasoning to coat evenly.

Serve immediately.

Delizioso!

Great as a kids brunch snack when adults are having a cooked breakfast!

Bacon & Cheese Popcorn

50g of popcorn kernels
1 tablespoon of butter
2 tablespoons of grated Parmesan cheese
A pinch of salt
2 rashers of bacon

Air pop popcorn using an air popper machine (see pages 15-18 for instructions), put in large bowl and set aside.

Grill bacon for three minutes on each side, or until crispy.

Once cool, cut into very small chunks.

Melt butter over low heat in a medium-sized pan.

In a bowl, mix the grated Parmesan cheese and add salt and stir in the melted butter.

Add bacon bits to the mixture and combine.

Spray popcorn lightly with cooking oil spray, add bacon/cheese mix and stir well. Eat at once!

Prawn Cocktail Popcorn

50g of popcorn kernels
1 bag of prawn crackers
Cooking oil spray

Air pop popcorn using an air popper machine (see pages 15-18 for instructions), put in large bowl and set aside.

Empty prawn crackers into food/freezer bag, seal and use rolling pin to crush.

Spray popcorn lightly with cooking oil spray and toss.

Sprinkle prawn crackers onto popcorn and mix well.

POP FACT:
Every popcorn kernel must be perfect to create popcorn! Even a small crack will let steam escape and the corn won't pop.

Caribbean Popcorn

50g of popcorn kernels
1 teaspoon of grated lemon zest
1 teaspoon of curry powder (mild)
A pinch of chilli powder (mild)

A pinch of ground pepper
2 teaspoons of desiccated coconut
1 teaspoon of icing sugar
Cooking oil spray

Air pop popcorn using an air popper machine (see pages 15-18 for instructions), put in large bowl and set aside.

Grate the lemon zest into a large bowl.

Add the curry powder, chilli powder, pepper, coconut and icing sugar and mix well – you now have your Caribbean seasoning.

Lightly spray the popcorn with cooking oil spray until it is covered and mix to coat evenly.

Sprinkle the seasoning over the popcorn and mix well.

Pizza Popcorn

50g of popcorn kernels
2 tablespoons of grated
   Parmesan cheese
$1/2$ teaspoon of garlic powder
$1/2$ teaspoon of Italian herb
   seasoning

1/2 teaspoon of paprika
1/2 teaspoon of sugar
A pinch of salt and pepper
Cooking oil spray

Air pop popcorn using an air popper machine (see pages 15-18 for instructions), put in large bowl and set aside.

Put grated Parmesan cheese into a bowl and mix in garlic powder, Italian herb seasoning, sugar, paprika, salt and pepper.

Spray popcorn lightly with cooking oil spray, and toss with seasoning to coat evenly.

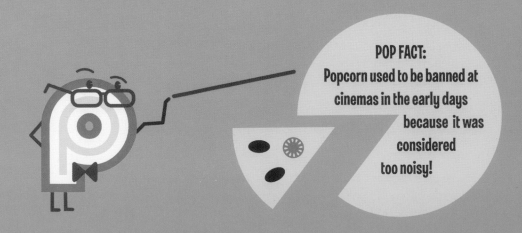

POP FACT:
Popcorn used to be banned at cinemas in the early days because it was considered too noisy!

(Spicy) Cheese Popcorn

50g of popcorn kernels
1 tablespoon of butter
$^1/_2$ teaspoon of paprika
A pinch of chilli powder
2 tablespoons of grated Parmesan cheese

Air pop popcorn using an air popper machine (see pages 15-18 for instructions), put in large bowl and set aside.

Melt the butter in medium saucepan over a low heat, then add the paprika, and chilli powder. Pour the butter mixture over the popcorn and stir to coat evenly. Turn the mixture into a lightly greased baking tin.

Bake at 130°C for 7 to 10 minutes, stirring once. The popcorn should become a little crispy.

Sprinkle with grated Parmesan and toss to coat evenly.

Let the popcorn rest, stirring once or twice as mixture cools, then serve.

About Peter Popple's Popcorn

Peter Popple's Popcorn was set up by Louise George and is a new healthy snack for kids and all the family.

Look out for Peter Popple's tasty range in good food shops, or buy it online at www.peterpopples.com. Peter Popple's Popcorn is made with only natural flavours and ingredients and is 'air popped', meaning it's cooked without using lots of oils. It comes in four family-friendly flavours: Cheddar Cheese, Salt & Vinegar, Fruit Chutney and Golden Syrup.

"There was a gap in the market for a balanced, fun, healthy and tasty snack. We have created a real alternative to crisps and regular salty snacks," says founder Louise George, "something that kids, mums, even dads would love – it's popalicious!"